mer

Menageri

EGUSI SOUP

JANICE OKOH

First performed at Mumford Theatre, Cambridge, on 18–19 May,
Soho Theatre, London, on 23 May–9 June,
Mercury Theatre, Colchester, on 14–16 June 2012

EGUSI SOUP

JANICE OKOH

Mrs Anyia	**Ellen Thomas**
Grace Olaleye	**Rhoda Ofori-Attah**
Anne Anyia	**Anniwaa Buachie**
Dele Olaleye	**Nick Oshikanlu**
Mr Emmanuel	**Lace Akpojaro**

Director	**Paul Bourne**
Producer	**Mhari Gallagher**
Set and Costume Design	**Louie Whitemore**
Lighting Design	**Paul Bourne**
Stage Manager	**Martha Mamo**
Cultural Adviser	**Funke Oyebanjo**

Thanks

Thanks to Patrick Morris, our Board of Trustees: Lester Lloyd-Reason, Alison Pearn, James Barlow and Nigel Atkinson, Nina Steiger for support with writer development, Sarah Dickenson for dramaturgy, Erin Gavaghan, Nick Dutton and everyone else at Soho Theatre, all at the Mercury Theatre, all at the Mumford Theatre, all at Eastern Angles, Taiwo Ajai-Lycett, Karlina Grace, Gracy Goldman, Sydney Smith, Lynette Clarke, Jason Okoh and Oscomms, Ray Barry, Gladys Okoh, all at Nick Hern Books.

LOTTERY FUNDED

Anglia Ruskin University, East Road, Cambridge

CAST

ELLEN THOMAS
Mrs Anyia

Awards include: twice nominated for Best Actress in the EMMA Awards; nominated as Best Actress by Screen Nation and the Black Media Awards.

Ellen has an extensive background in television, including the 2011 *Lenny Henry Christmas Special* and the inimitable Adoha in the BBC2 BAFTA award-winning *Rev*. In 2011 she joined the regular cast of the award-winning *EastEnders* to play the soap's first ever Nigerian matriarch Grace Olubunmi. She has also appeared in series four of *Teachers* and in two series of *Lenny Henry in Pieces*. Other regular roles include: three series of *Cardiac Arrest* and leading roles in *London Bridge*, *Holding On* and six episodes of *The Jury*. Ellen also appeared in *Buried Treasure*, which won the 2002 BAFTA Audience Award.

Other television credits include: *Come Fly With Me, Coming of Age, Moses Jones, Outnumbered, Bremner and Fortune, Little Miss Jocelyn, Trial and Retribution, The Marshioness Disaster, Never Never, Ultraviolet, Kavannagh QC III, Ruth Rendell's Simisola, Beck, French & Saunders, Hallelujah Anyhow*.

Film credits include: *Ashes, Clubbed, Breaking and Entering* directed by Anthony Minghella, *Basic Instinct 2: Risk Addiction, South West Nine,* Michael Winterbottom's *Wonderland* and *Secret Laughter of Women*.

Theatre credits include: various play readings for Tiata Delights, *Moon on a Rainbow Shawl* directed by Maya Angelou (Almeida); *Statement of Regret, The American Clock, Fuente Ovejuna* (National Theatre); *The Estate* (Soho); *Vagina Monologues* (tour); *Blest Be the Tie* (Royal Court); Maria in *Twelfth Night* (Manchester Royal Exchange); *A Bitter Herb* (Bristol Old Vic); *Amen Corner* (Tricycle/Nottingham Playhouse); *Echo in the Bone* (Women's Playhouse Trust at the Lyric Hammersmith); *Twelfth Night* (Birmingham Rep).

Radio credits include: *Say Goodbye Twice, Why is the Sky So Blue, Writing the Century, Statement of Regret, Claire in the Community, Silver Street, Face and Unspoken*.

Ellen also voiced 130 episodes of the popular children's series, *Jim Jam & Sunny* for Wish Films.

RHODA OFORI-ATTAH
Grace Olaleye

Rhoda trained at the Oxford School of Drama.

Theatre credits include: *A Doll's House* (Theatre Delicatessen); *Otieno* (Southwark Playhouse); *Romeo and Juliet* (Shakespeare's Globe); *In Time* (Almeida/Eastern Angles tour); *Word: Play 2* (Theatre503); *Molnar Shorts* (Finborough).

Television credits include: *Coronation Street, Arden of Faversham* for BBC's *Inside Out South East, Grownups Series II, The Bill, Rose and Maloney*.

ANNIWAA BUACHIE
Anne Anyia

Anniwaa won the Alan Bates 2007 Outstanding Newcomer Award.

Televison credits include: *EastEnders, Holby City, Spooks, Game Over.*

Theatre credits include: Lucky in *Waiting for Godot* directed by Matthew Lloyd (Tristan Bates); Anansi in *Anansi: An African Fairytale* directed by Lisa Cagnacci (Southwark Playhouse); Mrs Margret Abacha in *Work!* directed by Scott Le Crass (Theatre503); Woman in *The Cost of Things* directed by Caroline Steinbeis (Public Theater, New York); Aziza (Medea) in *Medea of Darfur* and Sabrina in *Sabrina* both directed by Shane Dempsey (Hackney Empire); June in *The Golden Hour* directed by Femi Elufowoju (Almeida/Tiata Fahodzi); Nana in *The President's Tobacco* directed by Kate Stafford (Young Vic); Serena in *Branded* directed by Matt Wilde (Old Vic).

NICK OSHIKANLU
Dele Olaleye

Nick trained at the Guildhall School of Music and Drama.

Theatre credits include: *Fixer* (Ovalhouse/Almeida); *Iya-Ile, The Estate* (Tiata Fahodzi/Soho); *Bulletproof Soul* (Birmingham Rep); *Crocodile Seeking Refuge* (Lyric Hammersmith); *The Gods Are Not To Blame* (Tiata Fahodzi/Arcola); *National Alien Office* (Riverside Studios); *References to Salvador Dali Make Me Hot, Gompers* (Arcola).

Television credits include: *Holby City, Silent Witness, Little Miss Jocelyn* (BBC).

Radio credits include: *A Long Journey, Playing Away* (BBC) and *Preserved of God* (Big Heart Media).

Nick has also assisted as a director and directed readings for acclaimed African theatre company, Tiata Fahodzi.

LACE AKPOJARO
Mr Emmanuel

Lace trained at the Identity Drama School.

Theatre credits include: *The Ladykillers* (Gielgud) in which his One-Round was described as a 'stand-out performance'; Bayo in *Torn* (Arcola); Rashad in *The Meeting* (Collective Artistes/national tour); Dad in *The Verdict* (Big Foot Theatre Company); Barnette Lloyd in *Crimes of the Heart* and Steve in *Small Craft Warnings* (Workhouse Theatre).

Television credits include: *EastEnders, Doctors, Rose and Maloney* and Bayo Adebanjo in the popular *Meet The Adebanjos.*

CREATIVE TEAM

JANICE OKOH
Writer

Theatre for Menagerie includes: *Introducing the Talented Mister* (monologue, Hotbed 2011).

In 2011 she won the Bruntwood Prize for Playwriting with her play *Three Birds* (*The Real House*) which was also shortlisted for the Verity Bargate and the Alfred Fagon Awards. In the same year she participated in the Channel 4 Scriptwriting Course.

Radio credits include: *SE8*, *From Lagos with Love*, *A Short Ride to Dusseldorf*, *Carnival* (part of the From Fact to Fiction series) and an adaptation of Malorie Blackman's cult novel *Noughts & Crosses* for the Saturday Play.

Current commissions include: Soho Theatre, Tricycle Theatre, Islington Community Theatre and BBC Radio 4.

PAUL BOURNE
Director

Freelance Director, Co-Artistic Director of Menagerie and the Hotbed Festival, Paul has directed and produced over seventy professional productions in ten different countries. His work has ranged from productions on the fringe through to major international touring. Highlights include: *Guignol* (Tennessee Williams) in New York and the UK; the world touring production of the *Complete Works of William Shakespeare Abridged* (out of Washington DC); and the European premieres of *Oleanna* and *The Secret Garden*.

Previously Artistic Director at the Frankfurt Playhouse and Center Stage New York, his focus is on commissioning, creating and developing new work for the stage. For Menagerie, he has directed plays by new and established writers including: Steve Waters, Fraser Grace, Judy Upton, Craig Baxter, Anna Reynolds and most recently Ed Harris. As Co-Artistic Director of the Hotbed Festival, Paul has commissioned over forty new pieces of work since the festival began in 2002. *Egusi Soup* was a piece that was first developed at Hotbed and it is great to see this debut play by Janice Okoh being produced following a long development journey.

MHARI GALLAGHER
Producer

Mhari has an MA in Theatre Direction: Text and Production from the University of East Anglia, which she passed with distinction.

Now working as a Freelance Producer, Director and Workshop Leader, recent projects include: producing support for Menagerie Theatre's Hotbed Festival (The Junction, Cambridge); the direction of *Kitchen Sink* (as part of the Hotbed Festival); the devising and direction of *The Lost Song* for Suffolk Arts Link; the design and delivery of the education programme for Scamp Theatre; the co-producing and co-direction of a 'Fall in Love with Theatre' event at the Mumford Theatre, Cambridge.

Previously, Mhari worked as the Associate Producer for Cambridge Arts Theatre. Credits include: *Guys and Dolls*, *My Fair Lady* and *Anything Goes*. Mhari also worked in the Marketing and Education departments at Cambridge Arts Theatre.

LOUIE WHITEMORE
Set and Costume Designer

Louie trained at Motley Theatre Design and the Royal Scottish Academy of Music and Drama.

Designing credits include: *Serse* (Iford Opera); *La Fille du Régiment* (Diva Opera); *Good Soul* (Young Vic); *I am a Superhero* (Old Vic New Voices at Theatre 503); *Mud* (Gate); Hotbed New Writing Festival (Soho/The Junction, Cambridge); *Hotel Medea* (Arcola); *The Adventure* (HighTide Festival); *Taniwha Thames*, *Measure for Measure*, *A Midsummer Night's Dream* (Ovalhouse); *Crossed Keys* (Eastern Angles); *Carmen* (Dorset Opera); *An Ideal Husband* (Heartbreak Productions); *Dracula*, (National Theatre); *Black Battles with Dogs*, *Summerfolk*, *Two Planks and a Passion*, *Much Ado About Nothing*, *The Winter's Tale*, *Figaro Gets Divorced*, *The Wild Duck*, *The Rehearsal*, *The Kitchen* (Cochrane); *Medea* (Platform Theatre); *The Magic Flute*, *Carmen*, *La Bohème*, *Albert Herring*, *The Marriage of Figaro* (costumes for Co-Opera Co); *The Tempest* (Sprite Productions); *The Bicycle Men* (King's Head); *Lucifer Saved* (Finborough); *Bed and Breakfast* (Underbelly); *The Bite of the Night* (Chandler Studios); *Twelfth Night* (The Arches, Glasgow).

As Associate Designer credits include: *The Nutcracker* (Shanghai Ballet); *The Nutcracker* (English National Ballet).

As Assistant Designer credits include: *Nabucco* (La Scala, Royal Opera); *Provincial Life* (National Theatre Wales); Mike Leigh Project (National Theatre); *Norma* (Grange Park Opera); *Alessandro* (Royal College of Music); *The Pearl Fishers*, *Turandot*, *Herodiade* (Dorset Opera); *Uncle Vanya* (Rose, Kingston).

Currently working on costumes for *The Messiah* for Danish Opera.

MARTHA MAMO
Stage Manager

Martha studied Stage Management at the Royal Welsh College of Music and Drama.

Theatre credits include: *Measure for Measure*, *The Heresy of Love* (RSC); *Realism*, *Mongrel Island* (Soho); *Ivan and the Dogs* (ATC/Soho); *The Painter* (Arcola); *Pieces of Vincent* (Arcola/Paines Plough); *Light Shining in Buckinghamshire* (Strawberry Vale); *Kursk* (Fuel/Young Vic/Sound and Fury); *Duet for One* (Almeida); *The Pride*, *A Miracle* (Royal Court); *Chess in Concert* (Heartache Productions); *Parade* (Donmar Warehouse); *Breathing Irregular*, *The Kreutzer Sonata* (Gate); *The Bull*, *Flowerbed* (Fabulous Beast); *The Changeling* (Cheek by Jowl); *Aladdin* (Old Vic); *One Flew Over the Cuckoo's Nest* (NiMax); *Julius Caesar*, *Dick Whittington* (BITE).

FUNKE OYEBANJO
Cultural Adviser

Funke is an inspirational and motivational script consultant, trainer and scriptwriter. After receiving her Masters in Screenwriting from the London College of Printing, she taught screenwriting seminars at various colleges and schools. She has worked extensively for the BBC, BBC World Service and the UK Film Council. She was one of the founder members of the Talawa Theatre writers' group and had her first play reading at Soho Theatre. Apart from having various shorts produced, her television script *The Window* was produced for Channel Four's Coming Up season. She also has three screen feature projects in development with a London based film company. One of her projects *The Land* was selected by the German based script development company, Script House for development at the Berlin Film Festival's talent campus and subsequently green lit by the Nigerian Film Corporation in 2011. She was selected as a juror for prestigious Skillset Creative and Innovative Award for Women in Television and Film. Currently, she is a Development Consultant with Arena Magica in Norway and one of the social commentators for the ongoing *Dotun Adebayo Show* and the *Eddie Nestor Rum Shop* on BBC London.

PRODUCERS

Menagerie Theatre Company

Menagerie Theatre Company was founded in 1999 by Paul Bourne, Patrick Morris and Rachel Aspinwall. Every year since then the company has produced at least one major new play for regional, national or international touring. Since 2002 the company has also produced an annual festival of new writing: the Hotbed Festival. Based in Cambridge, the company has a reputation for the discovery and development of writers through festivals, workshops, writers' schemes and support programmes. All of Menagerie's plays are commissioned or developed original works reflecting contemporary issues. Work has been shown extensively in the UK but also in the States, Turkey, Germany and most recently in India.

www.menagerietheatre.co.uk

Soho Theatre Company

Soho Theatre aims to bring the most entertaining, brave and theatrical new work to audiences across a programme spanning comedy, cabaret and theatre; with three spaces, a late-night bar, innovative education projects and world famous writers' centre, Soho Theatre is one of the most vibrant venues on London's cultural scene.

The Writers' Centre discovers and nurtures playwrights through a broad range of activity, developing their work towards production. Soho's accessible range of resources offers writers across the UK vital support at any stage of their careers.

www.sohotheatre.com

Colchester Mercury

The Mercury Theatre is a highly respected regional theatre and home to the critically acclaimed Mercury Theatre Company, staging a broad mix of classics and new writing as well as working extensively within the local community. Mercury Theatre Company – a company of actors, directors and creative artists, whose two core activities, work on stage and work engaging people of all ages and needs, remain of equal and vital importance. This company, unique in British theatre, remains innovative and challenging in its work and aspires to strive for regional, national and international collaboration and partnership, working and recognition.

www.mercurytheatre.co.uk

EGUSI SOUP

Janice Okoh

For my dad, Chief Hezekiah Chukuka Okoh, Ke-Alikwu
of Owaland (1929–2004)

Characters

ANNE ANYIA, *thirties, Nigerian, born and raised in England*

GRACE OLALEYE, *thirties, Nigerian, born and raised in England, Anne's younger sister, occasionally slips into a Nigerian accent when in her company*

MRS ANYIA, *fifties, Nigerian, attractive, mother to Anne and Grace*

DELE OLALEYE, *thirties, Nigerian, a bit sexy, husband of Grace*

MR EMMANUEL, *fifties, Nigerian, an out-of-work pastor of the Celestial Church of Christ*

Setting

A four-bedroom, mid-terrace house in South East London.

Note on Text

A forward slash (/) in the text indicates the point at which the next speaker interrupts.

This text went to press before the end of rehearsals and so may differ slightly from the play as performed.

ACT ONE

Scene One

Sitting room.

Stuck on the sitting-room wall with Blu-Tack, is a blown-up photograph of John Anyia, taken in his fifties, proud in traditional Nigerian dress. Beneath the photo the caption says: 'In Loving Memory of John Chucks Anyia 1945–2011'.

There are also other family photos: Mr and Mrs Anyia's wedding, the girls' graduation and one of John Anyia during a traditional religious ceremony. He has white-powder markings on him.

One armchair sits empty. This is John Anyia's chair.

Scattered about are four-pack cartons of UHT milk, a large boxed-up gasoline generator, two plastic wreaths and two overflowing suitcases.

MRS ANYIA *wears a black wrapper and T-shirt. These are her mourning clothes. On the front of the T-shirt is the same blown-up photo that is on the sitting-room wall.*

MRS ANYIA *finishes packing one of the cases. She tries to zip it up, some items fall out. She stuffs them back in and tries again. The exact same items fall out. She stuffs them back in, reties her wrapper and sits on the case.*

Enter GRACE. *She carries loads of bags. They look at each other.*

GRACE. We're gonna have to leave some stuff behind.

MRS ANYIA. Leave what? What can we leave? The generator? Small time now you will complain when there is no electricity. Or you want me to leave the flowers? Yes, leave the flowers and allow your father to lie in a bare grave. Come, sit on it. Sit. Sit.

GRACE *sits on the case.* MRS ANYIA *struggles to close it.*

GRACE. We're gonna break it.

MRS ANYIA. You are not even trying.

MRS ANYIA *gives up.*

I will have to use your suitcases.

GRACE. What?

MRS ANYIA. Are you going to use all your allowance? Dele will have space. He wears the same outfit day in and day out.

GRACE. He doesn't.

MRS ANYIA. Six days. I have counted.

GRACE. Those shell suits are from his consignment. They just need a bit of advertising. He's working on a brand name.

GRACE *gets up and starts to repack the case.*

MRS ANYIA. Remind your husband that we are undertaking your father's one-year memorial service, not the Nigerian *Apprentice.* Bring your suitcase.

GRACE. Mum, we need the space. His cousins want Xboxes and mobile phones.

MRS ANYIA. So he thinks this is a holiday we are going on?

GRACE. No.

MRS ANYIA. If he wants to dish out presents here and there he should do it in his own time.

A pause.

I hope you haven't invested your own money in these shell suits?

GRACE. Mum –

MRS ANYIA. You need to watch these boys. I am just advising you.

GRACE *pulls out a steering wheel from a car.*

GRACE. Who's this for?

MRS ANYIA. I promised Felix that I would bring it for him.

GRACE. Who's Felix?

MRS ANYIA. Felix has tiled the roof-now.

GRACE. What's this got to do with fixing the roof?

MRS ANYIA. Plenty. You have no concept of negotiation.

MRS ANYIA *stuffs the wheel back in the case.* GRACE *goes to the bags.*

GRACE. I suppose we can take these.

MRS ANYIA. So you have room?

GRACE. If we take out some of our / clothes.

MRS ANYIA. If you have room, can't you manage this?

MRS ANYIA *pushes the boxed generator towards* GRACE.

GRACE. Mum, that's the size of a suitcase.

MRS ANYIA. Why do you exaggerate?

GRACE. Fine. Fine. I'll take it.

MRS ANYIA *takes the gold outfits out of the bags and examines them.*

MRS ANYIA. Let me see what this woman has done. *Kai!* She didn't machine it well.

MRS ANYIA *measures the outfit against* GRACE.

Not well at all. Anne is much taller. Slimmer. You will have to take them back.

GRACE. Let's just wait.

MRS ANYIA. For what?

She is coming. And she says she has something important to tell us.

GRACE. Like what?

MRS ANYIA. Let us wait and see.

GRACE. Something important. That's just like her. Everything has to be big. Dramatic.

Enter DELE *and* MR EMMANUEL. *They wear the white robes of the Celestial Church of Christ. They are in jovial spirits.*

MRS ANYIA *brightens. Becomes just that tiny bit more 'feminine'.*

Welcome.

MRS ANYIA. Welcome.

MR EMMANUEL. Madam!

GRACE *helps* DELE *disrobe. Underneath,* DELE *wears a shell suit with the 'brand name' printed on it.* MRS ANYIA *takes* MR EMMANUEL's *robes. Underneath,* MR EMMANUEL *wears an immaculate but dated suit.*

GRACE. Pastor, would you like something to drink?

MR EMMANUEL's *phone goes off. He holds up his hand and answers it.*

MR EMMANUEL. I was expecting your call, ma. *Ehen… Ehen… Ehen…* This is because you have not been doing as I have said. Tonight before bed, drop a small amount of anointing oil onto a piece of paper, write down the names of all your enemies and stand on it. Yes. And this is how I want you to pray: 'Lord, let the enemies of my life destiny become a ladder for me to get to the top. Amen.' Repeat this every ten-ten minutes for half an hour. Then fold this paper and throw it away. That is why it has failed. You must throw it away. Text me tomorrow before twelve.

MR EMMANUEL *hangs up.*

You missed a wonderful day, ma.

MRS ANYIA. What time do I have to pray?

MR EMMANUEL. This is why you have daughters. To make time.

MRS ANYIA. Next time.

MR EMMANUEL. Next time. Next time. With you it is always next time. (*To* GRACE.) I hope you have been helping your mother-o.

MRS ANYIA. She tries.

MR EMMANUEL. Do you know there is an art to packing? When I was travelling to Philadelphia, I carried a suitcase this size – (*Indicates a tiny one.*) yet I managed to pack my entire wardrobe inside. Fifteen shirts in addition to the hangers.

DELE (*to* GRACE). You should have been there. The pastor said something very interesting. Uncle, what did he say?

MR EMMANUEL. He said, and this is an exact quote: 'Wives must try and do everything in their power to keep their husbands from straying. Therefore they should all travel to Deptford High Street to buy very nice black transparent underwear.'

MRS ANYIA. What pastor has said this?

MR EMMANUEL. This one pastor from Elephant and Castle-side.

MRS ANYIA. And what if the wife strays?

MR EMMANUEL. He suggested that the husband should also wear nice black transparent underwear.

MRS ANYIA. He is not serious.

DELE. This is what he said!

MRS ANYIA. Dele, go and bring your suitcase.

DELE. And then Mrs Adetoyin announced that she is pregnant.

GRACE. You are joking!

DELE. After five years of trying! All because of this man. (*To* MR EMMANUEL.) They are saying that Pastor Michael is losing his touch.

MR EMMANUEL. Pastor Michael is an experienced man.

DELE. You are too modest.

MRS ANYIA. Dele –

DELE. Yes, ma.

MRS ANYIA. Please, the suitcase.

Exit DELE.

MR EMMANUEL *goes to sit in John Anyia's chair.*

GRACE / MRS ANYIA. Pastor –

MR EMMANUEL. Oh, yes.

DELE *and* GRACE *make room.* MR EMMANUEL *sits elsewhere.*

So, the one-year memorial service! One year! What time is the prodigal daughter arriving?

GRACE. We don't know.

MRS ANYIA. Any time now.

MR EMMANUEL. I hope I am to greet this girl?

MRS ANYIA. Won't you be eating with us?

MR EMMANUEL. Have I been invited?

MRS ANYIA. Since when do you need inviting?

They laugh.

MR EMMANUEL. *Kai!* I thought this girl was bringing Supermalt?

MRS ANYIA. Yes, where are the drinks?

Exit GRACE.

MR EMMANUEL. So, now that your prayers have been answered –

MRS ANYIA. We do not know yet that they have been answered.

Enter DELE *with an empty suitcase.*

MR EMMANUEL. I know. Ma, we must praise Him for the things that He does just as often as we pray for the things that we want. Come for half the day. You will have such a wonderful time. Singing, dancing. Yes, dancing. Dele, you have been telling her about the dancing?

DELE. I tell her.

MR EMMANUEL. It is better than buying membership to Fitness First.

MRS ANYIA. Perhaps when you are pastor there. I am not sure of this pastor with his underwear advice.

MR EMMANUEL *receives a text.*

MR EMMANUEL. This is not yet finished.

He reads the text then texts back. MRS ANYIA *continues packing.*

Enter GRACE *with a tray of soft drinks.*

GRACE *and* DELE *continue packing. They put the generator in the case and lift the case onto the scales.*

DELE (*to* GRACE). So we are only taking three cases between us?

GRACE. She needs the space.

MRS ANYIA. How much does it weigh?

DELE (*to* GRACE). Raise your side. Fifty-one.

MRS ANYIA. Oh God!

DELE and GRACE *take the case off the scales and unpack it. By now* MR EMMANUEL *has finished texting and watches them.*

MR EMMANUEL. Thirty kilos. Everything must be thirty kilos. What respectable Nigerian who has not travelled home in how many months arrives at Gatwick with bags less than thirty kilos?

DELE. Did Ma tell you what happened the last time?

MRS ANYIA. Forget about last time.

MR EMMANUEL. Nigerians pack, pack, packing at the airport. Making the place look like a refugee camp.

DELE. There was this woman –

MRS ANYIA. Forget about this woman.

DELE. Pastor, this woman –

MRS ANYIA. I could see by her headscarf she was dodgy. Yoruba. From Kentish Town.

DELE. She offered to carry some packages for us.

MRS ANYIA. So kind.

DELE. So we accepted. How many times did we see her on the flight? As many as / eight –

MRS ANYIA. As many as eight or nine! And then we reached Lagos.

DELE. Gone.

MRS ANYIA. As if by magic.

DELE. 419!

MR EMMANUEL. *Kai!* That is the problem with Nigerians nowadays. The Indians, the Jews, they would never 419 each other.

MRS ANYIA. Nigerians? An Igbo would never have stolen from me. A widow carrying her husband home as cargo.

DELE. No, an Igbo would have stolen the package from you and then try to sell it back.

GRACE. Dele!

> DELE *laughs and picks up a case. It bursts. The entire contents fall out.*

> *Everyone starts talking over each other as they sort it out.*

You broke the zip!

DELE. Did I touch it?

MRS ANYIA. Bring your other case.

DELE. And what will we use?

GRACE. I'll have to go back down the high street.

MRS ANYIA. What of the dresses?

GRACE. They're fine.

MRS ANYIA. They will not size her! And what of Mrs Ebite's packages?

DELE. Who is Mrs Ebite?

GRACE. Let's just go.

DELE. So she is taking goods for someone else?

MRS ANYIA. And this girl will be arriving!

GRACE. Dele –

DELE. What of my / shell suits?

MRS ANYIA. I haven't even started the soup!

GRACE. I'll do it when we get back, Mum. Just finish this. Dele, come on.

MRS ANYIA. *Yemeke.*

> DELE *and* GRACE *put on their coats. They exit.*

> MRS ANYIA *resumes packing.*

MR EMMANUEL. The Igbos and the Yorubas…

MRS ANYIA. I was not talking of you.

MR EMMANUEL. Ma, in God's eyes we are all made equal.

MRS ANYIA. But He takes some before others.

MR EMMANUEL. He has His reasons.

MRS ANYIA. What reasons? My husband was a good man. Without any vice.

MR EMMANUEL. Every man has a vice.

MRS ANYIA. The pools. They still send him the coupons. He is disappearing.

MR EMMANUEL. He is here, Ma. In your two daughters. And how great they are! A *barristah* and a – a –

MRS ANYIA. With whom do I celebrate this greatness, pastor? Friends? Friends who have stopped visiting? In their twos, laughing, joking how we used to laugh and joke?

MR EMMANUEL. So come to our church. You will be surprised who you will find there.

MRS ANYIA. Strangers.

MR EMMANUEL. Who will become friends.

A pause.

MRS ANYIA. Let me start the soup.

MR EMMANUEL. Isn't Grace the one making it?

MRS ANYIA. This girl! I know this girl will add too much peppe.

Exit MRS ANYIA.

MR EMMANUEL *looks around the sitting room. He goes to sit down in John's chair but suddenly remembers and sits elsewhere.*

Scene Two

A few hours later.

Sitting room.

Enter ANNE.

ANNE. Hi! Hello?

Silence.

Hello?

*She wheels in a posh little suitcase and takes off her coat.
She wears casual travel wear underneath, designer. She
hangs it up, examines* MR EMMANUEL's *and* DELE's
white robes.

*She clocks the blown-up photo. John Anyia's eyes follow her.
It's a bit spooky.*

*She approaches his chair, touches it then sits in it, perhaps
takes off her shoes.*

Enter MR EMMANUEL *from upstairs.* ANNE *gets up.*

MR EMMANUEL. The big *barristah*! Welcome.

ANNE. Who are you?

MR EMMANUEL. I am a friend of your mother. Welcome.

ANNE. Where is she?

MR EMMANUEL. She has gone to look for more meat.

*He sits down. Drinks some Supermalt. He is very much at
home.*

Was your flight well?

ANNE. Yes, thanks.

MR EMMANUEL. Very good. *Ehen!* I am so sorry for your loss.

ANNE. Thank you.

A pause.

MR EMMANUEL. So! The big *barristah*! Your mother has spoken so much about you.

So much! You know, your father was very proud of you.

ANNE. I'm sorry, who are you again?

MR EMMANUEL *gets a call.*

MR EMMANUEL. *Ehen!* Excuse me. (*Into the phone.*) *Ehen. Ehen.* Okay. Tomorrow, you must read Matthew chapter seven, verse seven, and fast the entire day, telling God exactly what it is you want. Okay, if you are diabetic, fast until two. I will text you tomorrow.

He hangs up.

Let me introduce myself. My name is Pastor Emmanuel. I belong to an affiliation of the Celestial Church of Christ.

ANNE. I don't think I've heard of it.

MR EMMANUEL. It is very popular. Do you attend church?

ANNE. No.

MR EMMANUEL. Now is the time to start. So! The US of A. What a wonderful country. I travelled there many-many years ago. 'Have a nice day.' 'Have a nice day.' What a nice feeling to know that so many people want you to have such a nice day.

The front door opens.

Ehen!

GRACE (*off*). You should've called us. We could have got it.

MRS ANYIA (*off*). I have done it now. And it's two meats each, Dele, not five or six.

DELE (*off*). I will contribute to the meat.

MRS ANYIA (*off*). With what money?

DELE (*off*). I have money.

GRACE (*off*). Dele –

Enter MRS ANYIA *and* GRACE. DELE *carries in a brand-new suitcase. He can barely see from behind it.*

ANNE *opens her arms for a hug.*

ANNE. Hello, Mum.

Instead of hugging her, MRS ANYIA *dances up to and around her in celebration.*

MRS ANYIA. Heh! Heh! Heh! Finally you are here! Finally you are here! My daughter is finally here!

ANNE. You look well.

MRS ANYIA. Are you mad? When did you arrive?

ANNE. Just a minute ago.

MR EMMANUEL. The estranged daughter!

ANNE. I'm not estranged.

MRS ANYIA. You have met the pastor?

MR EMMANUEL. We have met.

DELE. I am Dele. Welcome.

ANNE is surprised by DELE's *appearance but she quickly hides it.*

ANNE. Nice to meet you. Congratulations. Your wedding. The both of you. I'm sorry I couldn't make it.

DELE. Forget it. We have plenty of photos for you to look at.

MRS ANYIA. Photos? What of the DVD?

ANNE. A DVD! Well, that's better than the real thing, isn't it? Crowded pop concert at Wembley Arena or watching it in the comfort of your own living room?

GRACE. Six people and a registry office is hardly Wembley.

ANNE. You know what I mean.

MRS ANYIA. So is it just you?

ANNE. Course it's just me.

MRS ANYIA *looks to* MR EMMANUEL *for answers.*

Presents!

ANNE *gets them out – a bunch of novelty pens – and hands them round.*

The Statue of Liberty goes up and down.

There isn't a pen for MR EMMANUEL.

Sorry.

GRACE. Have mine.

MRS ANYIA. It is a gift-now. Do you know these were the exact gifts we distributed at your father's funeral? I wish you had seen them. It was your father's face that travelled up and down. They went like hotcakes.

A very long pause.

ANNE. Oh.

ANNE *gets out her purse, counts out some cash, and gives it to* MRS ANYIA.

MRS ANYIA. It is too much.

MR EMMANUEL. God bless her! She is a good girl!

MRS ANYIA. Such a good girl.

ANNE *gives an envelope to* DELE. *He opens it.*

ANNE. It's for both of you. Dubai. First class. All inclusive. Money to spend of course. You'll love Dubai, Grace. The service is so amazing you don't feel guilty. It's like the waiters there really enjoy doing it.

GRACE. Thanks.

ANNE. I thought about getting you tickets to New York but it's not really honeymoony, is it? But to visit, you'd love it. It's so – Guess who I was having lunch next to the other day? Guess? Guess?

GRACE. I don't know.

ANNE. Guess?

MR EMMANUEL. Barack Obama?

ANNE. Monica from *Friends*. New York's like that. Celebrity everywhere. So how've you been, Grace? How's work?

GRACE. The same.

ANNE. I emailed. Guess you've been busy.

MRS ANYIA brings out a T-shirt identical to the one she is wearing and gives it to ANNE.

MRS ANYIA. Here. Put it on. Put it on-now.

ANNE puts it on, reluctant. It's just too painful.

Doesn't he feel close to your heart?

ANNE. Yes.

MRS ANYIA. This is the last one.

ANNE. Then you have it.

MRS ANYIA. I have been saving it for you. Sit! Sit!

Everyone goes to sit. ANNE goes to sit in John Anyia's chair.

MRS ANYIA / GRACE. No, not there.

ANNE sits elsewhere.

MRS ANYIA. You missed a very fine funeral.

MR EMMANUEL. Very fine! Who does not want to be buried back home with the scent of orange trees warming their tombstone?

DELE hands her a DVD.

DELE. I have burned you a copy.

ANNE. Is this the wedding?

MRS ANYIA. That is funeral-now. His final breaths, the wake keeping, the burial. All of it.

GRACE. You can watch it in the comfort of your living room. You know, just like Wembley.

MRS ANYIA. So what of the announcement?

ANNE. Well, it's not really an announcement. I just want to say I'm –

MRS ANYIA. You are getting married.

MR EMMANUEL. Hallelujah!

ANNE. What?

MRS ANYIA. I knew it!

ANNE. No! Who said anything about marriage?

MRS ANYIA *looks at* MR EMMANUEL.

MR EMMANUEL. Is there at least a husband on the horizon?

MRS ANYIA. You said you were seeing this boy.

ANNE. That ended months ago.

MRS ANYIA. You didn't tell me.

ANNE. It wasn't – It's not important. What's important is that I'm going to be here with you. For as long as you need me.

MRS ANYIA. What of your job?

ANNE. I'm taking time off. I'm owed it. I haven't had a day off sick in years and I never really take holidays. Anyway, that's enough about me. I want to hear about you. What you've all been up to, where you've been –

She looks at all the luggage.

Where have you been?

A pause.

GRACE. You didn't tell her.

MRS ANYIA. Of course I told her.

ANNE. Told me what?

DELE. Nigeria.

ANNE. What about it?

DELE. We are all going. For the memorial service.

ANNE. But you've already been.

GRACE. That was for the funeral.

MRS ANYIA. I told her!

ANNE. When?

MRS ANYIA. When you called-now!

GRACE. Maybe she was too busy to remember.

ANNE. I would have remembered. I would have remembered you saying / it was Nigeria.

MRS ANYIA. You said you were coming for his memorial service.

ANNE. Yes! Coming here! Home.

MRS ANYIA. That is home!

GRACE. Is it a problem?

ANNE. No, it's not a / problem.

GRACE. If you can't go –

MR EMMANUEL. Of course she will go!

GRACE. She might have to go back to work.

ANNE. I won't.

MRS ANYIA. She has time off. Hasn't she just said?

MR EMMANUEL. *Ehen!*

MRS ANYIA. I hope it is the one suitcase you are carrying because I will need to use your allowance.

GRACE. She hasn't got a ticket.

ANNE. I'll get one.

GRACE. If there are any left.

MRS ANYIA. She is a *barristah*. She will get one. Dele, help her with her case.

DELE *picks up* ANNE's *case*.

ANNE. So when are we going?

GRACE. Tomorrow.

ANNE. Fine.

Exit ANNE *and* DELE.

GRACE. Right. Well, I'd better see to the soup!

GRACE *exits*. MRS ANYIA *deflates*.

MR EMMANUEL. The *barristah* is here.

MRS ANYIA. With what? Novelty pens? She was supposed to bring a lawyer or a doctor. Even a teacher would have been okay.

MR EMMANUEL. These things take time, Ma.

MRS ANYIA. Pastor, the funeral was a mess. For his one year I wanted something to show that John Anyia was a success. That his enemies did not beat him down. That he is alive in his family. What family? You said she would bring a husband.

MR EMMANUEL. And she will. It is just a matter of when. But now that I have met this girl I know exactly how to pray for her. And this girl needs praying for. Now, where is the olive oil?

MRS ANYIA. I don't know.

MR EMMANUEL. It is okay. I have my own.

MR EMMANUEL *gets a mini bottle or hip flask of olive oil out from his jacket.*

It's hard for me to pray for you if you have one leg in and one leg out.

MR EMMANUEL *takes her hands and they both kneel down together.* MR EMMANUEL *places his hand on her forehead.*

Now, tell me what it is you want, Ma. What is it you want?

Scene Three

A few hours later.

The study overflows with John Anyia's things. Clothes, books, papers, his life.

The lights are off.

Enter GRACE. *She closes the door. Listens for a bit.*

She retrieves a jewellery box from the wardrobe, opens it, takes out a packet, pops a pill and puts the packet back.

The sound of a text coming through.

ANNE *is half-hidden on the floor in the corner of the room.*

GRACE *is not sure what* ANNE *has seen.*

ANNE. Hey.

A pause.

I've got you all upgrades.

GRACE. What?

ANNE. There was only business class left so I thought what the hell. We can all sit together. She didn't say anything about it, you know.

GRACE. Well, you've sorted it now, haven't you?

ANNE. God, the heart of bloody darkness! Just wish it was somewhere more convenient. Or at least with a tourist industry. Remember the last time we went? Remember? We took those taxis from Lagos to the village and the door handle came off in my hand? Remember? You didn't want to get in but Dad made you and there were no seatbelts. We shat ourselves the whole six hours. Remember? 'I don't wanna die before I'm famous!' God, that was funny.

A pause.

So… Married. Wow…

GRACE. We should go downstairs.

GRACE *moves things about, tidies up like that's what she came in the room to do.*

ANNE. I'd at least like to know something about him.

GRACE. She doesn't like any of it being touched. His things.

ANNE. I'm sorry. I couldn't get reception in my room.

GRACE. It's not me you need to be apologising to.

A pause.

ANNE. Dele seems nice. Where's he from?

GRACE. Nigeria.

ANNE. Okay. And where did you meet?

GRACE *rolls her eyes.*

It's gonna be three fucking long weeks if you're / gonna be like –

GRACE. It won't be if you stay out my way.

ANNE. You were the one who came in here.

GRACE. I didn't know you were here.

ANNE. Evidently!

A pause.

Look, your marriage is none of my business, fine, but I'm
gonna have to speak to him, aren't I? It's just simple –

GRACE. Work. We met at work.

ANNE. That's great. So, what, is he in telesales, too?

GRACE. He's a businessman.

ANNE. Oh, right. Doing what?

GRACE. Import, export. His business is doing really well,
actually. We're only here because Mum needs us. We'll be
moving out when we get back.

ANNE. Oh, right.

GRACE. Walthamstow. She doesn't know yet so don't say
anything. We want to break it to her gently.

A pause.

ANNE. Well, he sounds great. Really cool and –

GRACE. What?

ANNE. Nothing. I'm happy for you. Really.

A pause.

GRACE. So you seeing anyone?

ANNE. No.

GRACE. So you're still dating white.

ANNE. I'm single because I want to be. And there aren't any
black men in my circles. Or ones that'd be interested. I'm
not gonna defend myself. And it's not like you never did it.

GRACE. Once. The smell put me off.

ANNE. What smell?

GRACE. The milky, wet-dog smell.

ANNE. They don't / smell.

GRACE. And they're feeble.

ANNE. Let's just respect each other's tastes –

GRACE. Taste? What happened to being in your circles?

ANNE. Look, if the people I connect with happen to be white –

GRACE. You only connect with people like you –

ANNE. Dele's not exactly like you –

GRACE. Dele's like coming home, Anne. / You should try it.

ANNE. Coming home means you shouldn't have to change.

GRACE. I haven't changed.

ANNE. You might as well carry that on your head you're so ethnic.

GRACE. If you mean I'm comfortable –

ANNE. And you've got an accent.

GRACE. What accent?

ANNE. Whatever. I'm happy for you. Really.

GRACE. So you keep saying.

ANNE. Just as long as you're sure.

GRACE. He's not after a passport, we have a laugh and he's good in bed.

ANNE. Fine.

A pause.

He looks a bit like Dad, though.

GRACE. No he doesn't!

ANNE. A younger version.

GRACE. That's sick. You're sick!

Enter DELE. *They both look at him.*

DELE. Mummy would like to know when dinner will be ready.

GRACE. In a few minutes.

He exits slowly with the feeling that he's being talked about.

ANNE. It's around the eyes.

GRACE. Shut up! I mean, don't you think if he looked like
Dad, Mum or someone would've said?

ANNE. You're right.

GRACE. It's not funny.

ANNE. I know it's not funny.

GRACE. It's sick.

ANNE. Fine. I'm sorry.

A pause.

So, what's it like? The DVD? I mean, is he dead in it or is
he, you know, actually dying?

GRACE. He's dead.

ANNE. And you've all watched it?

GRACE. Yes.

A pause.

ANNE. What does he look like?

GRACE. Small. A bit like Lenin.

ANNE. Lenin?

GRACE. He looks like Dad, Anne. What do you think?

ANNE. I don't know. I don't know what to think. It's all a bit
creepy.

GRACE. It's what they do.

A pause.

The headstone broke. She tell you? We ordered one with his
name on it and a marble picture. It split down the middle as
they carried it over to the grave. They'd sold us a wad of
cheap cement.

ANNE. So why go back to all that aggro? Why not have something more meaningful here? We could clear this place out. All this stuff, we could give it away.

GRACE. Do you even care that he's dead?

ANNE. Of course I care. I didn't mean – You're right. This should be about Mum. What she needs.

GRACE. Yeah? So what exactly did she need when it actually happened?

ANNE. I was going for partner. They knew that.

GRACE. But you didn't get it.

ANNE. It was what Dad wanted. Look, I don't want to argue, Grace. All I want is to help.

GRACE. I just don't get what it is you want to do one year after the event.

ANNE. There isn't a limitation period on grief, Grace. She clearly needs someone to talk to.

GRACE. You're going to talk with Mum?

ANNE. Yes.

GRACE. About what?

ANNE. Politics. Things. It'll be organic.

GRACE. Well, I talk with Mum and we don't exactly talk about the current economic crisis. We talk about Dad. Correction, I listen to her talk about Dad. Going on and on at me because I'm not doing things the way he did them.

ANNE. Okay.

GRACE. Going through every detail of her life with him, telling me how much I don't understand what it's like to lose someone like I haven't / lost someone.

ANNE. Okay! Okay!

GRACE. Is it? Because you haven't once asked me about it. What it felt like.

ANNE. I don't need this.

GRACE. And I thought this wasn't about you?

ANNE. Okay, I'm sorry. I'm sorry I wasn't there. I'm sorry I left you to do it all. It was wrong, okay? Can't we just start again? Please? I want to help. I do. Just give me something to do. Something, you know, low-key. Or whatever you want is fine.

A pause.

GRACE. The speech.

ANNE. The speech?

GRACE. You're the big *barristah*. You should do it.

ANNE. The speech. Right. That's fine. That's great.

A pause.

GRACE. We'd better go down.

GRACE *waits for* ANNE *to get up and leave the room.*

ANNE. I really did want to come back for your wedding, Grace. Planned a whole day out beforehand. Just us. Shopping. Dinner. Wine. Actually, I brought us a bottle. Sancerre. Your favourite.

GRACE. I don't drink.

Exit ANNE *and then* GRACE.

Scene Four

MRS ANYIA, ANNE, GRACE, MR EMMANUEL *and* DELE
stand around the dining-room table. MR EMMANUEL *says
grace.*

MR EMMANUEL. We thank you for this bountiful food which
we are about to eat. For the hard work that has gone into the
preparation of this bountiful food. For the chopping of the
leaves, the pounding of the rice and the lighting of the gas.
We thank you for our health. For without it we would not be
here to eat this bountiful food that has been laid out for us.

ANNE. Amen.

MR EMMANUEL. Let us pray now for those who have
departed. That one day we will all be able to sit down and eat
together at this table once more.

MRS ANYIA / DELE / GRACE. Amen.

MR EMMANUEL. But not in the too-near future.

MRS ANYIA / DELE / GRACE. Amen.

MR EMMANUEL. We pray for this trip on which your children
are about to embark. That they will have safe journey. That
the plane won't be short of fuel. That the pilot is alert and
rested. That the runway will be smooth for landing. That the
red-eyed devils who wish evil on this family will be struck
down hard.

MRS ANYIA / DELE / GRACE. Amen!

MR EMMANUEL. We pray that this one-year celebration of
the passing of John Chucks Anyia will be a most successful
one. That his spirit will look kindly down on his daughter,
Grace, and make her blessed with a future generation of sons
to continue the Anyia name.

DELE. The Olaleye name.

MR EMMANUEL. Pardon?

DELE. We will be continuing the Olaleye name.

MR EMMANUEL. *Ehen*, the Olaleye name. Finally, we pray for your daughter, *barristah* Anyia.

MRS ANYIA. Amen.

MR EMMANUEL. That you will banish any troubles that she has.

MRS ANYIA. Amen.

MR EMMANUEL. That this trip will be fruitful for her.

MRS ANYIA. Amen.

MR EMMANUEL. That she will dress well, dance well, make herself up well-well and find a nice boy to settle down with.

MRS ANYIA. Amen.

> MR EMMANUEL *squirts some water at* ANNE *from a bottle*.

ANNE. Hey!

MRS ANYIA. It's just holy water.

MR EMMANUEL. Amen. Amen. Amen. Amen.

MRS ANYIA / DELE / GRACE. Amen.

> *Everyone sits.*

> *The following conversation plays as* GRACE *serves the ground rice and soup in the order of* MR EMMANUEL, DELE, MRS ANYIA, ANNE, *herself.*

> *They eat in silence.* ANNE *sniffs and drinks water as they eat.* GRACE, DELE, MRS ANYIA *and* MR EMMANUEL *have no reaction.*

DELE. Seeing us giving thanks like this must be a surprise for you.

ANNE. No, it's fine.

DELE. So you pray?

MR EMMANUEL. She doesn't but I will pray for her.

ANNE. I thought you just did?

MR EMMANUEL. That was only the start. On your return, Grace will bring you to our church.

ANNE. Wait, you go to the Celestial Church of whatsits?

DELE. It is the Celestial Church of Christ.

ANNE. Aren't they those barefooted lot in the white smocks that hang by the Costcutters?

DELE. Our church is situated above it.

ANNE (*to* MRS ANYIA). Do you go as well?

MRS ANYIA. Well, I –

MR EMMANUEL. On your return from Nigeria you will all go.

ANNE. It's not really for me. But thanks.

MR EMMANUEL. Do you know how many men you will find there? Yoruba, Igbos, white. They all come there. It is the new internet dating.

GRACE. Is the soup tasting okay?

MR EMMANUEL. It's wonderful. Very wonderful. (*To* ANNE.) You must always give thanks. Remember, it is prayer that has brought you this your success.

MRS ANYIA. Amen.

MR EMMANUEL. It is prayer that will bring Grace her children.

MRS ANYIA. A child would have been the icing on the cake. To have paraded him through the village.

DELE. It will soon happen.

MRS ANYIA. Soon. Always soon. I hope your eggs are not rotten.

ANNE. Mum, maybe she doesn't / want –

GRACE. I can speak for myself.

ANNE. Yeah, I know but –

GRACE. But nothing.

A pause.

MR EMMANUEL. You know it was prayer that found Dele his new job – (*Mispronouncing her name, which he continues to do.*) Anne.

ANNE. It's Anne.

MRS ANYIA. You remember how he refused to take it?

DELE. I refused because I didn't know what the job was.

MRS ANYIA. 'I have an MBA. I have an MBA.' How many people hold MBAs and PhDs in the same hand as vacuum cleaners! There is no shame in cleaning. Do you know how many menial jobs my husband took so that he could purchase this house?

ANNE. You're a cleaner?

GRACE. His main thing is his business.

DELE. Wahala Fashion. It is my brand. Wahala.

DELE *hands* ANNE *a business card.*

MRS ANYIA. He is a cleaner.

DELE. I am a manager. I manage four sites.

MRS ANYIA. Which have to be cleaned by you twice a day.

DELE. 'Yes, Mr Olaleye. No, Mr Olaleye.' Or sometimes they just call me boss. I prefer boss but I don't want them to think that I am their boss. The number-one rule of management is to let them believe that they are your friend. Is that not correct?

ANNE. I'm more banking, acquisition finance, that sort of stuff.

MR EMMANUEL. So you will be able to advise me. I recently purchased a car from this one woman in Manchester –

ANNE. I know nothing about consumer law. I'm in acquisition finance.

MR EMMANUEL. Did I not use finance to acquire the car?

ANNE (*to* MRS ANYIA). So, when did you all start going to this church?

DELE. You have a problem?

ANNE. No. No –

MRS ANYIA. Their father did not encourage religion.

MR EMMANUEL. Perhaps if he had had a small piece of faith...

ANNE. You think praying would have – ?

MR EMMANUEL. Prayer would have stopped it in its tracks.

ANNE. He had cancer.

DELE. It wasn't cancer. It was poison.

ANNE. If that's what you want to call cancer –

MR EMMANUEL. Cancer is what they say to explain what they can't explain.

ANNE. Are you serious?

MRS ANYIA. Your father had many enemies. Jealous people.

MR EMMANUEL. People who are not aware that England is not a bed of roses.

ANNE *looks at* MRS ANYIA *and* GRACE.

ANNE. So you think they poisoned him?

DELE. They put something in his soup.

ANNE. Who?

DELE. His enemies.

ANNE. And you have proof?

DELE. He is dead-now.

ANNE. This is – Grace – ?

GRACE. If you believe something is real then it's real.

ANNE. Oh, right. I must have missed those lessons at school. You know, the ones on juju and witchcraft.

DELE. It is no joke. I had this one room-mate, Tunde. An A-star student who never once studied! Not at all. We had heard things about him. He carried this small-small pouch round his neck. This pouch he never took off. One day when he was sleeping, we opened the pouch...

MRS ANYIA. God forbid!

DELE. A child's finger.

MR EMMANUEL. *Kai!*

DELE. The child could not have been more than three years old.

ANNE. That doesn't mean something like that happened to Dad.

DELE, MR EMMANUEL, GRACE *and* MRS ANYIA *all look at her.*

GRACE. Pastor, is that all the meat you are having? There is plenty there.

MR EMMANUEL. Thank you.

They resume eating in silence. ANNE *sniffs. Sips more water.*

GRACE. You don't have to eat it, you know.

ANNE. It's fine.

MR EMMANUEL. You know, Anne, the entire village will be attending the church. There will be plenty of men for you to choose from.

ANNE. Sorry?

MR EMMANUEL. Why not kill two birds with one rock?

ANNE. I'm not just going to bring a man back. There's a thing such as love, you know.

DELE. So we do not love each other?

ANNE. No, I didn't mean –

MR EMMANUEL. A traditional marriage is what your father would have wanted.

ANNE. How would you know what he would have wanted?

DELE. He knew Daddy-now. They worked together at Midland Bank.

MR EMMANUEL. We were in security. In those days jobs flew about like dry leaves around your ankles. We were never in any one place for long. I met your father and I said to myself: this man will go very far. He succeeded, Anne. Through his daughters. A *barristah* and Grace is a – a –

MRS ANYIA. She could have been an engineer!

MR EMMANUEL. An engineer!

GRACE. Mum –

MRS ANYIA. Are you becoming one of those lesbians?

ANNE. No! I've had boyfriends!

MRS ANYIA. But they have all failed. If only you would wear lipstick.

ANNE. As if that's gonna get me a man!

MRS ANYIA. I was the best-dressed girl in the village. I was not necessarily the prettiest but still your father had no choice but to select me. You see, he thought he was doing the selecting but in truth I was the one selecting.

ANNE. Mum, I'm not going there to be paraded about.

MR EMMANUEL. But this is the reason you are going.

MRS ANYIA. And when a nice boy sees you are up there speeching, advertising your big, big career –

MR EMMANUEL. She can speak her language?

MRS ANYIA. She cannot speak it.

MR EMMANUEL. Why Nigerians born and raised here cannot speak their native language? The Indians, the Chinese, they all speak two, three – *Comment appelez-vous*? Yes-now! French. I lived there for three years before travelling to Ireland.

MRS ANYIA. What were you doing in Ireland?

MR EMMANUEL. Just finding my way.

MRS ANYIA. To where?

MR EMMANUEL. Into England. I was known as the international traveller. There are so many men back home, Anne. Educated ones like Dele. You should take the time to look.

DELE *sucks his bone, making a loud noise.*

It is prayer that will bring you a good Nigerian.

ANNE. Pastor, I don't want –

MR EMMANUEL. You need a good Nigerian husband.

ANNE. I'm not marrying someone from the bush!

DELE. The bush?

ANNE. I mean uneducated.

DELE. I have an MBA.

ANNE. Yes. / I know, sorry.

DELE. A Masters in Business Administration.

MR EMMANUEL. Anne, you must ask yourself why it is that Grace is married to a very fine man and you are not.

ANNE. Who the fuck is this guy?

MRS ANYIA. Oh God!

ANNE. I'm sorry, I didn't mean to –

It's too much for her and she downs her glass of water.

MRS ANYIA. Pastor, sorry-o.

MR EMMANUEL. I am used to these kind of girls.

MRS ANYIA. I should have sent them home to be educated. Their father wanted to but I refused. (*To* ANNE.) That is why all these English men you like prefer these Eastern European women. Do these women talk and swear like a man? Who would want to come home to that mouth?

MR EMMANUEL. What your father wanted was for you to be settled like your sister.

GRACE (*to* DELE). *So fé si.*

DELE *passes his plate up to* GRACE *for more.*

MR EMMANUEL. You must marry before it is too late. You are no spring chicken. It is what your father wanted.

MRS ANYIA. And grandchildren.

MR EMMANUEL. *Ehen!*

DELE. And we will parade them at the five-year anniversary.

MRS ANYIA. Five years.

DELE. Daddy will not be lost, Ma. He will never be lost.

MR EMMANUEL. As long as you have faith.

DELE. Amen.

Scene Five

Bedroom. Same evening.

DELE *and* GRACE *undress and get into bed.*

DELE. The bush? The bush?

GRACE. Okay.

DELE. Who does she think she is? With all the 'she is in this country, she is in that country, she is having lunch with Veronica from *Friends.*'

GRACE. It's Monica from *Friends.*

DELE. Does she know I am related to the king of my village? That I am royalty. Does she know that?

GRACE. No.

DELE. We don't boast about these things. But if you are from our place you can tell by just looking at me. It is in the shape of my forehead. What a mouth! She talks like she is on *Jeremy Kyle. Kai!* If she was representing me in court I would be very worried.

GRACE. She doesn't go to court.

DELE. God is good!

DELE *laughs.*

Did you see her face? Did you see it? When I told her about the pastor and Daddy? She looked like she had smelt shit.

GRACE. Alright.

DELE. There's too much peppe!!

GRACE. Dele –

DELE. Okay.

A pause.

Dubai! What do we want with Dubai?

GRACE. What will we do with the tickets?

DELE. We will sell them.

GRACE. But they are a gift-now.

DELE. We can use the money to invest. Yes! In Nollywood.

GRACE. Nollywood?

DELE. My cousin knows people out there.

GRACE. What cousin?

DELE. Elvis.

GRACE. Elvis!

DELE. What is wrong with Elvis?

GRACE. The motorbike you shipped over for him to sell last
    year is what is wrong. Where is the motorbike and where is
    the money?

DELE. I told you, someone 419'd him.

GRACE. Why don't we just go?

DELE. Go where?

GRACE. Dubai. We could relax in the sun, go shopping –

DELE. There is plenty sun in Nigeria. This here is our future.
    Our new place away from your mother's provocation.
    Money for our new business venture. Nollywood is booming
    but it is in distribution we will need to find the contacts.
    Distribution is a closed shop.

They are both thinking.

GRACE *snuggles into him.*

GRACE. This is nice.

DELE. Yes.

She kisses him. It starts to get passionate.

GRACE. Me, you, the beach, room service, baby oil…

DELE. Baby oil.

GRACE. So which one will we do?

DELE. Which one what?

GRACE. Are we staying or are we going?

DELE. We are going.

GRACE. Okay.

DELE. Going where?

GRACE. Dubai.

DELE. Yes. No. Yes. *Kai!* What am I agreeing to?

GRACE. It is just a holiday, Dele. Who knows? You might like it.

DELE. Things are very slow, Grace. I did not imagine my future here cleaning.

GRACE. The shell suits will sell. Would I have invested if I didn't believe it? Like the pastor says, you have to have faith.

DELE. It is your family.

GRACE. Thank you.

GRACE *switches the lights off.*

Goodnight.

DELE *switches the lights on.*

DELE. Weren't we starting something?

GRACE. We need to sleep.

DELE. We can sleep on the flight. I will do all the work.

GRACE. That's what you always say.

DELE. I can't stay like this.

GRACE. Okay. Be quick.

DELE. I do not dictate to my prince.

GRACE *gives in and* DELE *prepares to have sex.*

GRACE. Thought you were going to do all the work?

DELE *looks at her, confused.*

GRACE *indicates oral sex.*

DELE. I will do it after.

GRACE. There's a reason why it's called foreplay.

DELE *dives under the covers and gets to work. He comes back up.*

What's wrong?

DELE *jumps out of bed.*

DELE. I was saving it for Nigeria.

DELE *gets out a small bottle of white liquid.*

GRACE. What is it?

DELE. We put it on.

GRACE. And lick it off?

DELE. It is what Uncle Emmanuel gave to Mrs Adetoyin.

GRACE. Mrs Adetoyin?

DELE. He came to me again, Grace. I wish you had seen it. Pow. Pow. Pow. I was thrown from one direction to the next. Emmanuel had to pick up my chair it was so strong. It was telling me something is coming to us. To this house. A child is coming.

GRACE. I thought we were doing it naturally?

DELE. This is one hundred per cent natural ingredients.

GRACE. How much did it cost?

DELE. What is the price of conception?

GRACE. How much?

DELE. One twenty for a day's worth.

GRACE. One twenty?

DELE. Look at Mrs Adetoyin.

GRACE. Dele, we don't know what went on there.

DELE. The pastor knows. Close your eyes.

GRACE. Why?

DELE. Close your eyes, Grace. Please?

> GRACE *closes her eyes.* DELE *rubs in the lotion until he is completely white.*

Now, what do you imagine?

GRACE. I don't know.

DELE. Come on, imagine. When I close my eyes, I see it all. How we talked. We will have a boy first and we will call him Ekundayo. Ekundayo will keep an eye on our wayward daughter Ola and Mummy will curse me for giving them Yoruba names. I know you are losing faith but there is no need. The pastor says imagining is one step closer to achieving.

> GRACE *opens her eyes. She's shocked by his appearance.*

GRACE. Oh my God, Dele!

> DELE *takes a handful of dried corn kernels out of a bag and sprinkles it on the floor, around the bed. He starts scratching himself and continues to do so more frequently throughout the rest of the scene.*

What are you doing?

DELE. It will enhance the blessing.

GRACE. In what way?

DELE. Give it chance!

GRACE. It smells like chicken innards.

> DELE *takes it off her.*

DELE. You don't have to smell it. You need to put it inside you. Bend over.

GRACE. No way!

DELE. You have eaten and drunk everything else the pastor has blessed without complaint.

GRACE. Water and apples, Dele. This is –

DELE. This is what?

GRACE. This is definitely not a turn-on!

DELE. Isn't this what we want?

A pause.

GRACE *bends over.*

GRACE. So does it all go in or what?

DELE. It has to last three days.

GRACE. Three days?

DELE. It is a three-day course-now.

Itching and scratching, DELE *approaches with the potion.*

GRACE. Dele –

DELE. Quiet! You are making me spill it!

GRACE. Dele, your skin. Look at your skin. Wash it off, Dele. For fuck's sake, just wash it off!

DELE *heads for the bathroom, hopping painfully over the corn kernels.*

Exit DELE.

Jesus, Dele! And you wanted to put that inside me! Jesus!

GRACE *gathers up the corn kernels. She starts to cry but stops herself.*

And when he comes tomorrow, you're getting a refund!

Scene Six

Living room.

ANNE *is alone in the dark. She's drunk a glass or so of the Sancerre. She stares at the traditional portrait of John Chucks Anyia.*

Enter DELE. DELE *is still half-undressed and still has white on him.*

In the dark, the white on DELE *is luminous. He holds something similar to what John Chucks Anyia holds in the portrait.*

DELE *looks exactly like John in the religious ceremony photo.*

ANNE. Dad.

End of Act One.

ACT TWO

Scene Seven

Early, the next morning.

Sitting room.

ANNE *is still in the chair.*

Enter MRS ANYIA *with a packed suitcase. She is dressed in her traditional gold outfit. She looks amazing.*

MRS ANYIA *clocks the wine. She is not impressed.*

MRS ANYIA. You are not dressed.

> MRS ANYIA *finishes packing.*

Go and dress. The pastor will soon be here.

> *A pause.*

Anne.

> ANNE *picks up the bottle and glass and gets up.*

Is that what they taught you over there?

ANNE. It was one glass.

MRS ANYIA. You know your father never liked it.

ANNE (*re John's chair*). It looks so small now. Shrunken. I used to think it was so big. Me and Grace, sitting on the back of it picking his grey hairs. Half a P for five.

MRS ANYIA. You would beat her for her share.

ANNE. She beat me. Grace was the violent one. She just looks gentle.

> *A moment as they are lost in their own thoughts.*

MRS ANYIA. Let me show you something.

MRS ANYIA goes and sits in a chair.

Biah!

ANNE goes over and sits at MRS ANYIA's feet. She rests her head on MRS ANYIA's lap.

What are you doing?

ANNE. I just –

MRS ANYIA. It is paining me.

ANNE lifts her head. MRS ANYIA finds the remote and switches on the DVD player.

ANNE. What's this?

MRS ANYIA. The casket. The one you paid for.

ANNE. Mum, I don't –

MRS ANYIA. Maple wood. White with silver trimming. Zinc lined. The Majestic.

The entire village gathered around it like it was a bar of solid gold. It was a pity we had to bury it. Following him to the church. In cars. On *okada*. It was as if he was a king. Crying. Crying.

They both watch the video. MRS ANYIA derives great comfort from it.

ANNE. Something happened at work, Mum. Something – With that boy. At work. That boy I told you about.

A pause.

It was a mistake. I made a mistake.

A pause.

MRS ANYIA. Did Grace tell you about the headstone? It broke in two. Over the grave and the grave hadn't even been filled.

ANNE. Mum –

MRS ANYIA. That is bad luck.

ANNE. It was a difficult period. He'd just died and I –

MRS ANYIA. Help me understand it.

ANNE. Understand what?

MRS ANYIA. What is taking them so long! To make you partner. How many years working and nothing has changed when everyone else's children are consultants and surgeons? Mrs Wonoro has a politician. She looks just like Moira Stewart. You are going to tell me that you cannot go to Nigeria.

ANNE. But it's not because –

MRS ANYIA. You have to work.

ANNE. No. It's because of / this boy –

MRS ANYIA. They are calling you back.

ANNE. The one I told you about –

MRS ANYIA. But you have to say no.

ANNE. Mum –

MRS ANYIA. This time, you will say no.

ANNE. Mum, please?

MRS ANYIA. You will call them and tell them that this is more important. You are going to your father's one-year today and they will have to wait. You will tell them to wait. Honour your father and they will respect you.

A pause.

The front doorbell goes.

That is the pastor. Now go and get dressed.

ANNE *gets up and exits.*

MRS ANYIA *arranges her attire and answers the door.*

Welcome!

MR EMMANUEL *looks her up and down*.

MR EMMANUEL. *Ehen!* This is what I am talking about!
When you enter the village everyone will know that John
Chucks Anyia, Bachelor of Arts, was a success in this world.
They will say, 'Here are his three daughters. When did this
man produce three daughters?'

MRS ANYIA *laughs*.

MRS ANYIA. Would you like something to drink?

MR EMMANUEL. I hope you have Supermalt.

MRS ANYIA. Of course.

MR EMMANUEL. Is this all the luggage?

MRS ANYIA. This is it.

Exit MRS ANYIA.

MR EMMANUEL *flicks some holy water around the room
and on the luggage, murmuring a prayer all the while*.

Enter DELE *and* GRACE. *They wear the traditional gold
outfits*.

GRACE (*to* DELE). Go on then.

DELE. Let him finish.

MR EMMANUEL *finishes*. DELE *takes* MR EMMANUEL
aside. GRACE *listens in*.

Pastor, please, I want to talk to you about this small blessing –

MR EMMANUEL. So you have already started?

DELE. Yes. But I am not sure it is working.

MR EMMANUEL. It is a course-now.

DELE. What are the side effects?

GRACE. He had an allergic reaction.

DELE. Grace, I am managing this. (*To* MR EMMANUEL.) I
had an allergic reaction. See.

DELE *shows* MR EMMANUEL *his arms and body.*

MR EMMANUEL. Are you sure this is because of the blessing?

GRACE. He is sure.

DELE. Grace –

MR EMMANUEL. Not once on how many occasions have I done this has there been a problem!

GRACE. Pastor –

MR EMMANUEL. Someone is working against us.

DELE. Is it my university room-mate?

GRACE. Dele, this is not Tunde.

MR EMMANUEL. When you are close to getting what you want, evil like this will try to permeate. Listen well-well. When you are in Nigeria, make sure you monitor your dreams. And keep away from people who are close to you.

DELE. My relatives? You think I should not visit them.

MR EMMANUEL. These people come in different guises. Sometimes not even human.

GRACE. Pastor, it is a lot of money and we can't use the blessing.

MR EMMANUEL *brings out his wallet.*

DELE. Pastor, it is okay.

MR EMMANUEL *offers some money.*

MR EMMANUEL. No one should be dissatisfied.

DELE. Pastor –

MR EMMANUEL. I don't want argument here.

DELE. There is no argument.

GRACE. Dele –

DELE. *Jo! Jo! Jo!*

GRACE *moves off.*

MR EMMANUEL *puts his money away.* MRS ANYIA *enters with the drinks.*

MR EMMANUEL. Madam! What is your plan for when you arrive there?

MRS ANYIA. We will arrive in Lagos and from there we will drive straight to the village. We have advertised so the villagers will all be congregating.

MR EMMANUEL. Stage one!

MRS ANYIA. Of course-now!

MR EMMANUEL. I see it all! You, parading in all your finery, followed by John Chucks' identical twin sisters. One is very fat. Fair skin. The other is skinny-skinny.

MRS ANYIA. You have seen the DVD!

MR EMMANUEL. When have I seen it? His sisters will be followed by the professional mourners.

MRS ANYIA. They have only been invited for the Sunday as they outstay their welcome.

MR EMMANUEL. Then there will be dancing.

MRS ANYIA. A live band.

MR EMMANUEL. Yes, I see it.

MRS ANYIA. Iron Lady!

MR EMMANUEL. I cannot hear.

MRS ANYIA. Let him hear. Dele! Bring the CD.

DELE *finds the CD and puts it on.*

As his wife, I will dance first. Followed by my husband's children. And then his sisters and their children.

MR EMMANUEL. There will be no wickedness here!

Delighted, MRS ANYIA *starts to dance. She does, slowly at first, becoming swept up in the music.*

MRS ANYIA. Then Grace and Dele will follow. Dance-now!

MRS ANYIA forces GRACE *and* DELE *to dance but they are still annoyed with one another.*

MRS ANYIA picks up the Post-it Notes from the table and, pretending that they are money, puts them on her own forehead, one by one. One by one, the Post-its fall to the ground.

And they will spray me and my daughters who will pick the money. Are you seeing? Dele, Grace, pick the money.

DELE *and* GRACE *pick up the Post-its.*

And they will remember him and dance for him and eat for him. They will eat for John Chucks Anyia!

Enter ANNE. *She wears the traditional gold outfit. Her headscarf is wonky.*

MR EMMANUEL. *Ehen!* So you are a traditional woman at last!

MRS ANYIA. *Biah! Biah!*

MR EMMANUEL. She is calling you.

MRS ANYIA. You need to practise. The entire village will be watching. Waiting to criticise. Waiting to slander his name.

MR EMMANUEL. Can she dance or are her hips made of cement?

MRS ANYIA dances beautifully, moving her shoulders agilely and in time to the music, like a twenty-year-old. As she dances, she looks at MR EMMANUEL *several times in the hope that he is watching her in admiration, just like how she imagines the whole world will be. He is.*

You see your mother? This is how it is done!

MR EMMANUEL *dances with* MRS ANYIA.

GRACE *and* DELE *start dancing with each other.*

MRS ANYIA. Do you know Iron Lady is coming to Agbor especially for this event?

MR EMMANUEL. Because he is great.

MRS ANYIA. He is great! Anne, *biah*!

She grabs ANNE, *pulls* ANNE *towards her.*

ANNE. Mum, don't –

MR EMMANUEL. When I preached in Catford –

MRS ANYIA. You preached in Catford?

MR EMMANUEL. Yes-now! I had my own church but it was converted into flats.

MRS ANYIA. Sorry-o.

MRS ANYIA sprays ANNE *with the Post-its.*

MR EMMANUEL. God has his plan.

MRS ANYIA. He has his plan!

ANNE. Stop it.

MRS ANYIA. I am showing the pastor what will happen.

MR EMMANUEL. I know-now! It is your daughter who has never been home.

ANNE. I've been home.

MR EMMANUEL. So you know that you should be spraying the whole village.

MRS ANYIA. She will be paying for the cows.

MR EMMANUEL. Is that all? She is a big *barristah*!

ANNE. Mum, stop it.

MRS ANYIA continues spraying her.

I'm not going.

MRS ANYIA. Pardon?

ANNE. I'm not going.

DELE switches off the CD.

MRS ANYIA. Why?

ANNE. Because they sacked me, Mum. They sacked me.

A pause.

For seeing that guy, that paralegal. He was just there.
Twenty-six with these big blue eyes – I just needed some
comfort after he died.

GRACE. Anne –

ANNE. I wanted to come home but they didn't like it. I told
you. They don't like weakness. Not from partner material.
They said I was partner material. Anyway, I knew what that
jumped-up Oxbridge wannabe wanted. I knew it all along.
Hideous monster. That's how he described me. In the email. I
got it by mistake. I don't know what made me scroll down.
Anyway, I tried to get rid of him. You have no idea how hard
it is to get anyone sacked nowadays. You complain. Follow
the normal procedures but they just get moved around and
around and you keep bumping into them in the lift. You get
one of the those saggy-bellied white lawyers screwing
around and it's pats on the back, dick-comparing, ball-
holding bragging but I do it and I get dismissed. Go on then,
tell me it's my fault, Mum. Tell me that I'm stupid. So
stupid. I'm a stupid, ugly, stupid, big-lipped, flat-nosed,
small-tittied, narrow-hipped, thick-waisted, flat-footed, stiff-
ankled, dry-handed, picky-haired ugly black bitch!

A silence.

MRS ANYIA. Why do you have to do this now?

GRACE. Mum –

MRS ANYIA. Embarrassing your father.

ANNE. Did you even hear me?

MRS ANYIA. Hear what? What?

MR EMMANUEL. This girl's head is not correct.

MRS ANYIA. She has always been selfish.

ANNE. Really? Cos whenever you want something, Mum, I
pay. Repatriation, I paid. When he asked for money to build
the house – the Mercedes, who bought it? Who bought it?
All I wanted – I just wanted –

ANNE *heads for the exit.*

MRS ANYIA. Where are you going?

GRACE. Anne!

ANNE. What's the point?

MRS ANYIA. He asked for you. Before he went. And you said
you were coming. You said you were coming to the man who
paid for your education. Made you what you are. Watching
small boys pass over him. White boys, but he took it. He
took it all for you and you think you have repaid him?
Money here and there? Expecting me to feel sorry for you
because of this white boy you chased like some pub
prostitute? Losing your job? No. You get ready. *Oiya!* You
get ready to travel to Nigeria and honour him. You will
honour him like he deserved. You will honour him.

Exit ANNE. GRACE *follows.*

Scene Eight

Sitting room.

Shortly afterwards.

MR EMMANUEL (*on phone*). *Ehen! Ehen!* Every day, before
you go out, I want you to anoint yourself with virgin olive
oil. Virgin olive oil. Yes, Tesco's is okay but not the value
price. Then turn around three times. *Ehen.* Your son will
serve no more than six months. Text me again before ten.

He hangs up. He waits. Enter DELE.

What is happening here?

DELE. Do I know?

MR EMMANUEL. Go and enquire-now! I have another engagement.

DELE *prepares to go.*

Be very careful that she does not influence your wife.

DELE. Grace will not be influenced.

MR EMMANUEL. But she has not been coming to church.

DELE. This is because – Pastor, I beg, advise me. She is against the blessing, my plans for Nollywood –

MR EMMANUEL. Nollywood?

DELE. Wahala films. I am looking to produce.

MR EMMANUEL. If you need an actor, I have taken part in a documentary for the terrestrial channels.

A pause.

What is the problem?

DELE. Pastor, we do not want the same things.

MR EMMANUEL. She is an English girl-now.

DELE. I know she is English!

MR EMMANUEL. Look around you. What do you see?

DELE *looks around.*

Where is the other man?

DELE. What other man?

MR EMMANUEL. There is no other man. This is my point. This man is gone. Dele, you are the one who makes the decisions. You are the one who should be obeyed. A woman without a man is like egusi soup without egusi. There is plenty there but this soup is nothing without its sweet flavour. And we want our women to have flavour. Are you the flavour?

DELE. I am the sweet flavour. So what do I do?

MR EMMANUEL. Dele, you must tell your wife to listen. Tell her to listen well-well.

DELE. To listen?

MR EMMANUEL. Yes-now! Because that is what they all want to do.

A pause.

DELE *heads towards the exit, unsure.*

Ehen!

Exit DELE.

Scene Nine

Study.

ANNE *and* GRACE *sit in silence.*

ANNE. I sort of feel relieved. Being wheeled about. I never liked it. Being the best. I blame my GCSEs. Maybe if I'd have failed some. All his fucking hopes.

GRACE. Can't believe they sacked you.

ANNE. Indefinite leave.

GRACE. Which means they can call you back?

ANNE. There was a tribunal, Grace. Everything. They're not gonna call me back.

GRACE. Well, at least now you know what they're like.

ANNE. And they know what I'm like. If I get another job it's gonna be on less pay and it's gonna take me even longer to be partner.

GRACE. Well, fuck 'em.

ANNE. I can't just fuck them, Grace. It's my whole life.

GRACE. So instead you're gonna be treated like shit?

ANNE. It's the city. It's what it's like. Anyway, it's what Dad would want.

GRACE. You think?

ANNE. It's all he ever talked about.

GRACE. Not at the end. You didn't know him at the end.

A pause.

ANNE. I saw him, Grace. Last night. He came to me. Like a vision. Right there and then –

GRACE. You saw him?

ANNE. All white, like the photo.

GRACE. I thought you didn't believe in all that?

DELE *comes to the door. They do not see him.*

ANNE. I know but then that happened, Grace. To me. I know what he wants.

A pause.

GRACE. You just can't have it, can you?

ANNE. What?

GRACE. You can't have it that I was with him at the end. That I was the one who really knew him. No, you have to do one better. You have to go and see his ghost.

ANNE. I didn't mean –

GRACE. Well, it wasn't Dad, Anne. It wasn't him.

ANNE. I know what I saw.

GRACE. It was Dele.

ANNE. Dele?

A pause.

Why was he all white?

GRACE. It doesn't matter.

ANNE. Go on, if it was Dele –

GRACE. It's not the point.

ANNE. It is if you're / trying to –

GRACE. It was a fertility rite!

ANNE. A fertility rite?

GRACE. Yes.

ANNE. A fertility rite? But you're –

GRACE. I know! On the pill.

A pause.

ANNE. I was going to say educated.

A pause.

GRACE. Well, at least it's out in the open cos I know you know, Anne.

ANNE. I know now. Now. Because you just told me.

A pause.

GRACE. I do love him, you know. Like sometimes my heart would burst. It's not lying. It's buying time.

A pause.

So, you gonna tell him?

ANNE. What happened to us, Grace?

GRACE. Exactly what you wanted to happen. What would have happened if they hadn't sacked you? If they hadn't sacked you, where would you be right now?

A pause.

ANNE. You have to tell him, Grace. If it's a proper marriage. A real / marriage.

GRACE. Of course it's a real marriage.

ANNE. Why are there all these secrets?

A pause.

DELE. Mummy wants to know if you are going.

A pause.

ANNE. Right. I'm – I'll just –

Exit ANNE.

A pause.

GRACE. She's not going. Told you she wouldn't go. I tried to talk her round but she – You packed? Cos if we haven't packed –

A long pause.

DELE. How long?

GRACE. I don't know what you – ?

DELE. How long have you been taking contraceptives?

A pause.

How –

GRACE. I'm not sure. Maybe a few weeks. Months.

DELE. And you discussed this with the woman who did not come to your wedding?

GRACE. No.

DELE. Who left you to watch your father poke his swollen ankles as his liver / failed him –

GRACE. I didn't tell / her.

DELE. Watch his chest turn hard as he pushed out / his last breath?

GRACE. She found them! I thought she did.

DELE. Where?

GRACE. It doesn't matter.

DELE. Where?

GRACE. In there.

> DELE *goes to the wardrobe.*

> Under the sheets.

> DELE *brings out the jewellery box. Opens it, looks inside.*

DELE. Where we come from, a man is respected. In our country, a man makes the decisions. He is obeyed. Are you the man? Are you the man?

GRACE. No.

DELE. I can't hear you.

GRACE. No.

DELE. You knew it wouldn't work. The blessing. And the pastor said someone close was working against me –

GRACE. The pastor! He'd say anything to keep you paying!

DELE. Shut up!

GRACE. All the blessings and prayers.

DELE. Shut up!

GRACE. He is a businessman! You of all people should see it. Don't you think it's strange? These visions everyone has. People stumbling about with one eye open in case they bash into each other? If you're so consumed by the angels, how come it's so clean? How come no one ever gets hurt?

DELE. So you think I am lying?

GRACE. No.

DELE. This is what you married. You knew this!

> *A pause.*

> From day one we talked about children, Grace. Planning. Is there another man?

GRACE. When would I have the time to see someone else?

DELE. I don't know, Grace. You stopped going to church. You are taking contraceptives.

GRACE. No.

DELE. Why should I believe you?

A pause.

GRACE. Dad used to bring home these sweets from work. He'd ask us in the morning what we wanted. She would say Nutty. I wanted Twix. It was always a Nutty that he'd bring home for us to share even though a Twix is already divided into two.

DELE. Twix, Nutty. What has this got to do with anything?

GRACE. You should have seen his face when I told him about you. A big, strong man. Educated. Traditional. He liked that. Traditional.

DELE. You married me to please your father?

GRACE. I don't know.

DELE. So what do you know? You have a husband. The chance of a family and you don't know. You want to be out there floundering about like your sister? Is that it?

GRACE. No.

DELE. Do you know, I see women like your sister on the train every day? Her friends are married with their children and the men she looks at won't look at her because she is too old and too much like them. Is that what you want? That life? Because they don't want it, Grace. They want this. They all want this. You girls born here see so many things on offer that in the end you are confused.

A pause.

Okay, so I will wait?

GRACE. You've got names for them.

DELE. Do you want me to wait?

GRACE. I don't know.

A pause.

DELE. You are scared. Is that what it is? You are scared?

GRACE. No.

DELE. You don't have to be scared.

GRACE. No.

DELE. Once you hold our child –

GRACE. No.

DELE. Then get away from me! Go on! Pack out!

A pause.

So what is it you want to do? If you don't want to have children, what are you going to fill up your time with?

GRACE. I don't know.

DELE. There must be something. New York, America. You must have planned something. Don't I deserve this?

GRACE. I don't know.

Scene Ten

Sitting room.

MRS ANYIA *watches* MR EMMANUEL *spray holy water around the living room.*

She musters up her courage and enters.

MRS ANYIA. You see what I have to deal with?

MR EMMANUEL. You have tried-now!

MRS ANYIA. Pastor, what do I do? Should she still go? If she goes, what will we say to his enemies?

MR EMMANUEL *suddenly stops. He convulses, throws himself about the room and shouts* 'Mimo, mimo, mimo!' *before collapsing onto the floor in a fit. He is suddenly still.* MRS ANYIA *goes to him.*

Pastor? Pastor! Oh God! Dele! Dele!

MR EMMANUEL *comes to.*

Are you okay?

MR EMMANUEL. What happened?

He resumes spraying holy water. He staggers about.

MRS ANYIA. Pastor, please, sit down. I thought you had a heart attack.

MR EMMANUEL. I have seen them. The angels.

MRS ANYIA. Will it be a good trip?

MR EMMANUEL. Yes. Although your daughter is beyond repair. Fortunately, you have another daughter.

MRS ANYIA. Yes.

MR EMMANUEL. But she will soon abandon you.

MRS ANYIA. Abandon me how?

MR EMMANUEL. She will be following her husband east-side.

MRS ANYIA. East-side?

MR EMMANUEL. Have they not discussed this with you? These children-o. This is where our church is moving. Do you have anyone who can drive you? The Tube station is very far from there. Or perhaps –

MRS ANYIA. Perhaps what?

MR EMMANUEL. I am not sure you are ready.

MRS ANYIA. Pastor, I am ready.

MR EMMANUEL. The angels are telling me to lay foundations here, Ma.

MRS ANYIA. Here?

MR EMMANUEL. In this house. It is a well-sized house. Very similar to the one I had in Catford. They are saying that when you return from your travels, you will be ready to cross different pastures. They are telling me many things.

He places his hand over hers.

MRS ANYIA. It has not been up to a year.

MR EMMANUEL. I have to do whatever I am called to do, Ma.

MRS ANYIA *removes her hand.*

MRS ANYIA. And I have to pack.

MR EMMANUEL. Yes! Where are these children? Dele! Grace!

MRS ANYIA. I will manage it.

MR EMMANUEL. I will come and visit as soon as you are back.

MRS ANYIA. There is no need. (*A pause.*) Do you know my husband did not have one day of illness? Not a single day. He always knew someone would do something. Whenever we went home I did all the cooking. He would never touch what the housegirl prepared. Different ones each time. But there are always people coming to the house, begging for favours. 'Someone's going to kill me. Someone's going to kill me.' That is all I ever heard from him. This strong man. I didn't believe it. Not really. I know they hated him and people could plot and plot but this was our house. I left it. The soup. I left it unattended. I was called out and I left it. For five minutes. We all ate it but he fell ill right after that. We left Nigeria the beginning of August. He was dead five weeks later. So I believed it. I believed that someone poisoned him. He died not because his body betrayed him, lied to him, pretended that it was well and then allowed the cancer to kill him, but because someone wicked simply wished it. It explained the injustice, the suddenness of it all. Yes, my husband worked in security, pastor, but never at Midland Bank.

MR EMMANUEL. There were many jobs at this time –

She opens the door for him.

MRS ANYIA. Thank you for all your help, pastor, thank you, but I don't need a church or any angels here. I will manage very fine on my own.

MR EMMANUEL. It will be a successful trip, Ma. Very successful. The angels, they have – [ordained it.]

MR EMMANUEL*'s phone rings. He answers on his way out.*

(*Into phone.*) I have been expecting your call. *Ehen! Ehen! Ehen!*

Exit MR EMMANUEL.

Scene Eleven

Sitting room.

MRS ANYIA *repacks some of the cases. Everywhere is a mess.*

Enter ANNE *with her packed suitcase. She's got some of her gold outfit on. Maybe just the top. They look at each other.*

MRS ANYIA *continues to pack.*

ANNE. I've got friends in Highgate. I can stay with them.

MRS ANYIA. If that is your decision.

ANNE. We're meant to be honouring him, Mum. We should honour him with the truth or what's the point? Where's the pastor?

MRS ANYIA. He has gone.

ANNE. Well, that's something.

MRS ANYIA. Since your daddy died, the pastor has been here every single day.

ANNE. I made a mistake, Mum. I should've come back. I'm sorry.

MRS ANYIA *continues packing. She can't zip the suitcase up. The zip breaks. She breaks down.* ANNE *doesn't know what to do. She approaches* MRS ANYIA, *who allows herself to be comforted for a moment but she's limp with it.*

MRS ANYIA. Thirty-six years. Together every hour, every minute. Walking together, sleeping. He was my skin.

MRS ANYIA *moves away from* ANNE *and carries on packing.*

ANNE. I thought I saw him, you know. Dad. Last night. For just a second. Looking just like that.

MRS ANYIA. What did he say?

ANNE. Nothing. But he was angry. Angry that I let him down. Well, I thought he was.

MRS ANYIA. He would have been angry.

A pause.

The pastor will no longer be coming here. He is moving eastside. I do not know how I will pack all of this.

A pause.

ANNE. Well, you've got to be practical for a start.

ANNE *repacks the luggage.*

You don't need that, that or that. Or that. Or any of that. Or that. Or that.

She brings out packets of Pampers, boxes of cereal, stacks and stacks of shoes and the steering wheel.

What the – ?

MRS ANYIA. I promised Felix.

ANNE. Who's Felix?

MRS ANYIA. The tiler.

ANNE. Oh, okay. For negotiation purposes.

ANNE repacks the steering wheel.

MRS ANYIA looks at ANNE *with new eyes.*

A honk of a taxi.

MRS ANYIA. Where is Grace? Grace!

ANNE goes to the front door.

ANNE (*shouts*). Five minutes, okay?

Enter GRACE. *She has changed out of the gold outfit.*

Where's Dele?

GRACE. He's upstairs. Mum, we're not going.

MRS ANYIA. Oh God!

ANNE takes away the cases so there are only two left.

GRACE. We've got things to talk about.

MRS ANYIA. Can't you talk on the plane?

GRACE. No.

MRS ANYIA. It is his one-year.

GRACE. I know.

A pause.

MRS ANYIA. So what is it that you two have to talk about?

GRACE. I don't know. Things.

MRS ANYIA. You'd better hurry up and know or do you want to end up like your sister? A reject? (*To* ANNE.) Sorry-o. (*To* GRACE.) Marriage is not a new dress you can discard when you have grown bored of it. You adjust. Take up the hem.

GRACE. You don't even like him.

MRS ANYIA. So he's Yoruba, but he is a good boy. Loyal.

(*To* ANNE.) Talk to her.

ANNE. I think I'm the last person to be giving relationship advice.

MRS ANYIA. Okay. Fine. Fine. Whatever you girls want.

MRS ANYIA *gets on with the packing.*

GRACE *and* ANNE *look at each other.* ANNE *brings back her suitcase and a spare so that there are now four to pack.*

MRS ANYIA *looks at her.*

ANNE. But I'm not giving the speech. And if anyone asks what I'm doing I'm telling the truth.

MRS ANYIA. Not the entire truth.

ANNE. Whatever feels right.

MRS ANYIA. Okay.

ANNE. Three weeks. Shit.

MRS ANYIA, ANNE *and* GRACE *start packing the four suitcases frantically, picking and choosing bits.*

GRACE. All you need to do is smile, genuflect to the old ones and don't touch anyone Mum doesn't know or let them touch you. If you think it's all rubbish, you risk it.

MRS ANYIA. What of Mrs Ebite's package?

ANNE. She can take them when she goes herself.

MRS ANYIA. But I promised her.

GRACE. The only time she's ever been round is to drop them off. She's got her own family.

ANNE. What's that box?

MRS ANYIA. The generator.

ANNE. Shit. Leave it. I've done India.

MRS ANYIA. Are you sure?

ANNE. We'll stay in a hotel.

The women pack in silence. MRS ANYIA *slows down, looks at her daughters.*

MRS ANYIA. I can't remember the last time we were all together like this.

ANNE. His sixtieth.

GRACE. The day after. You couldn't make it.

MRS ANYIA. Yes. We had the dinner the day after.

A pause.

ANNE. I called his mobile. Once. A few months after it happened. Listened to his voicemail message. It still worked.

MRS ANYIA. You listened to his voice?

ANNE. It didn't sound like him any more.

A pause.

GRACE. I put up photographs of him on my wall. At work. I thought he was beautiful after all the shit he went through. The ones of him in Nigeria weren't as good as he'd started to decompose by then.

ANNE. Your work allowed you to have pictures of a dead man on your wall?

GRACE. It was still Dad. Anyway, someone notified HR. I didn't know my employment package includes six Bupa telephone counselling sessions.

ANNE. I hope you used them.

GRACE. Maybe I should have eased away my pain by harassing a twenty-six-year-old.

ANNE. Maybe I should paint myself white when I'm trying for a kid.

MRS ANYIA. Who painted themselves white?

GRACE. Dele. It was a fertility rite.

MRS ANYIA. Fertility rites? Well, he is from the village.

GRACE. Is that all you have to say?

MRS ANYIA. What? You will never find someone who is one hundred per cent perfect, Grace. You have to adapt. Whatever it is, you overcome it.

A pause.

I hear that Felix has a son –

ANNE. Mum, please –

MRS ANYIA. Just wait until you meet him.

ANNE. I told you, I'm not interested in those types of men.

MRS ANYIA. A bird in the bush is worth nine.

ANNE. What?

MRS ANYIA. A bird in the bush is worth nine.

ANNE / GRACE. A bird in the hand is worth two in the bush.

MRS ANYIA. Yes-now!

ANNE *and* GRACE *catch themselves laughing together.*

I did not think your father was particularly handsome but he was very popular. Educated. And he had a moustache. With a space right here. How I loved this moustache. So sophisticated. He shaved it off soon after we were married. When I close my eyes I see him with that moustache. Just concentrate on one feature. With you everything is about the outside.

The sound of a car horn.

They all get up.

MRS ANYIA *approaches* GRACE, *her arms open.*

ANNE *and* GRACE *sort of laugh.*

Is this not what you girls want?

GRACE. I never wanted it.

ANNE. It looks a bit fake.

MRS ANYIA. Can I never do anything right?

GRACE. You're gonna be late.

ANNE. I'm gonna see him, aren't I? See his grave.

GRACE. Yeah. You got your passport?

MRS ANYIA *and* ANNE *check for them. They have them.*

The sound of a car horn.

MRS ANYIA. What is wrong with this boy?

MRS ANYIA, GRACE *and* ANNE *drag the four cases towards the door.* MRS ANYIA *pulls out the biggest bag ever.*

ANNE. What's that?

MRS ANYIA. Hand luggage.

ANNE. Mum, they're not going to allow that on the plane.

MRS ANYIA. They will allow it. *Oiya!*

ANNE. Mum –

MRS ANYIA. You are a big *barristah*. You will be able to make the unreasonable sound reasonable.

ANNE. What did I tell you about calling me that?

MRS ANYIA. Who knows what that is over there? You are a *barristah*. Why do you make things so complicated?

The women exit the house with the suitcases. The taxi drives off.

GRACE *enters.*

She tidies up. Then goes over to John Anyia's chair. She touches it as if she's touching him and then sits in it.

She looks at John Anyia's portrait.

Enter DELE. *They look at each other for a very long time.*

GRACE. I'll make us something to eat.

Dim lights.

End.

Glossary

Barristah	Lawyer
Biah	Come here
Ehen	Is that so? / That is so
Jo	Please (dismissive)
Kai	An exclamation.
Kiro	What's wrong?
Ma	Mother
Mimo	Holy
Oiya	Go
Okada	Motorbike taxis
So fe si	Would you like some more?
Yemeke	Thank you

Other Titles in this Series

A Nick Hern Book

Egusi Soup first published in Great Britain as a paperback original in 2012 by Nick Hern Books Limited, 14 Larden Road, London W3 7ST, in association with Menagerie Theatre Company

Cover photograph by Ray Barry
Cover design by Ned Hoste, 2H

Typeset by Nick Hern Books, London
Printed in the UK by Mimeo Ltd, Huntingdon, Cambridgeshire PE29 6XX

A CIP catalogue record for this book is available from the British Library

ISBN 978 1 84842 271 1

MIX
Paper from
responsible sources
FSC® C019549